This Book Belongs To:

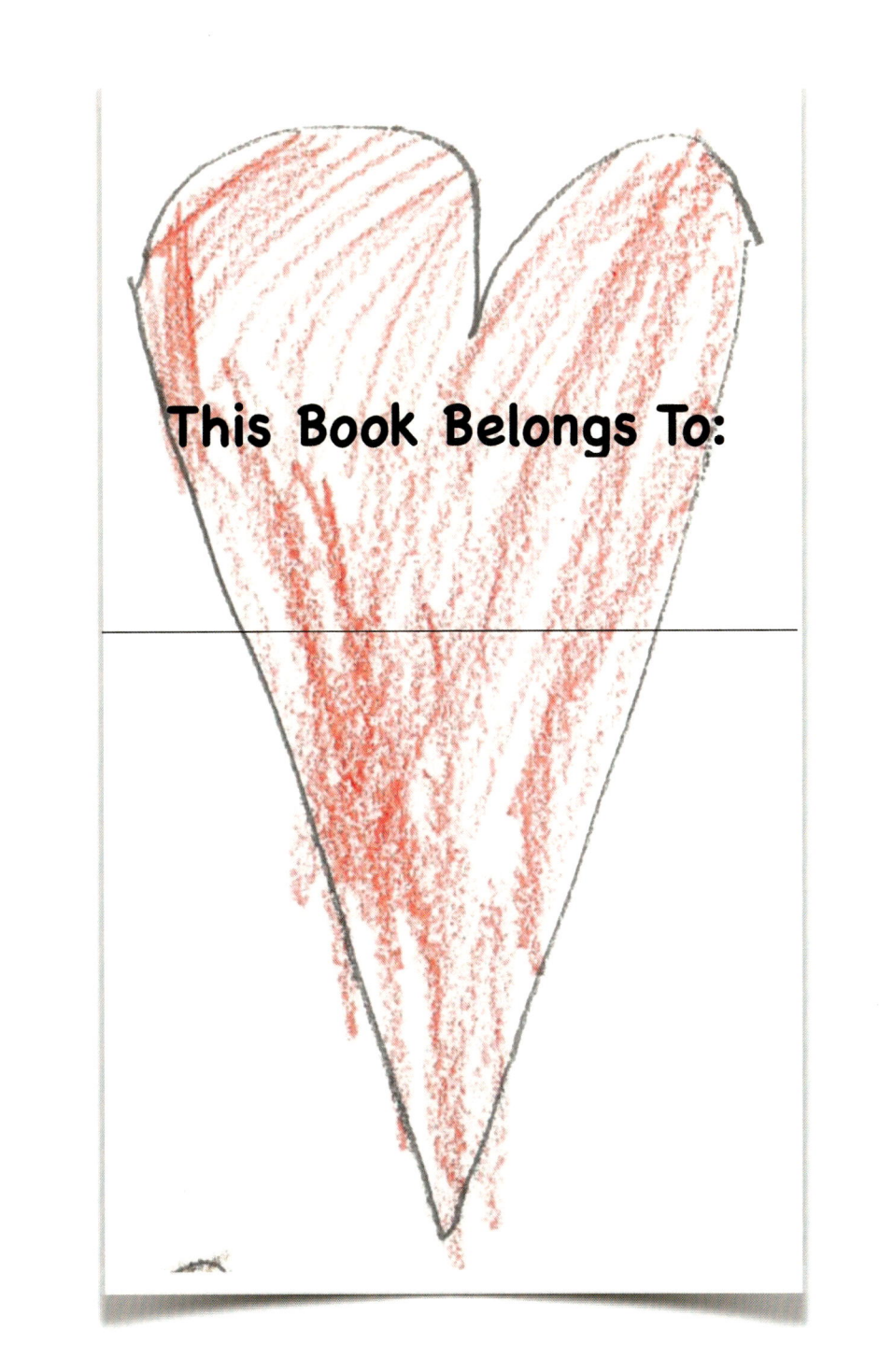

Because of Love

Text copyright © 2020 by Damitra Newsome
Illustrations copyright © 2020 by Kaycie Newsome

SoAllMayKnow Publishing
P O Box 6718
Largo, MD 20792

soallmayknow@gmail.com

SoAllMayKnow
PUBLISHING ™

All rights reserved. No parts of this book may be reproduced, transmitted, or stored in an information retrieval system in any form or by any means without prior written permission from the author, except as provided by the United States of America copyright law.

Unless otherwise noted, all Scripture quotations are taken from the Holy Bible, New International Reader's Version®, NirV®. Copyright © 1995, 1996, 1998, 2014 by Biblical, Inc.™ Used by permission of Zondervan. www.zondervan.com The "NirV" and "New International Reader's Version" are trademarks registered in the United States Patent and Trademark Office by Biblical, Inc.™

Scripture quotations marked as NLT are taken from the *Holy Bible*, New Living Translation, copyright © 1996, 2004, 2015 by Tyndale House Foundation. Used by permission of Tyndale House Publishers, Inc., Carol Stream, Illinois 60188. All rights reserved.

ISBN 978-1-7347064-2-0

Cover design by Caretha F. Crawford

Cover images & background interior images credit: iStockphoto

Printed in the United States of America

Because of Love

Damitra Newsome

Illustrated by Kaycie Newsome

SoAllMayKnow PUBLISHING™

ACKNOWLEDGMENTS

I want to thank my husband, Kenneth Newsome, Jr., for his continued support of my many endeavors and my daughter, Kaycie Newsome, for her compassion and energy that continues to motivate me. I want to acknowledge, my Pastor, Melvin Anderson, who gave our family an assignment that led to the development of this book. In addition, I want to thank my mother, Audrey Jackson, and my late father, Jerry Jackson, for always encouraging me to set goals and stick with them even amid adversity and setbacks. They always reminded me of the goals I set and met along the way. And I want to thank God, my Heavenly Father, for sticking with me, being patient with me, and most of all, for loving me and showing me His great love for all humankind.

PROLOGUE: Message from the Author

"Because of Love" is a story of mercy, compassion, sacrifice, obedience, and love. You see, humankind had strayed far from God, His true love, and continued to disobey Him. We were in need of a Savior. And there just weren't enough animals in the world to sacrifice for all of our sins.

So our great and awesome God put into action a plan to save us all. This amazing plan can be read in the gospels of Matthew, Mark, Luke, and John. What you will find there is a story of a man named Jesus who came to save the world. More than the story of the greatest man's life, it is the ultimate love story about God's power to save us through His Son, Jesus.

"Because of Love" is a very short version of that story. It is written through the eyes of a child for their understanding of God's great love for His people. As you read, I hope you will see just how much God loves you.

Damitra Newsome

This is how Jesus the Messiah was born. His mother, Mary, was engaged to be married to Joseph. But before the marriage took place, while she was still a virgin, she became pregnant through the power of the Holy Spirit.

Matthew 1:18 NLT

Because of LOVE...

Mary had a Baby named Jesus by the power of the Holy Spirit.

Because of LOVE...

Shepherds and wise men visited young Jesus after His birth. They worshipped Him and gave Him gifts.

Then they opened their treasure chests and gave him gifts of gold, frankincense, and myrrh.

Matthew 2:11b NLT

There the child grew up healthy and strong. He was filled with wisdom, and God's favor was on him.

Luke 2:40 NLT

Because of LOVE...

Joseph and Mary cared for their Son, Jesus, and took Him to the temple of the Lord.

Because of LOVE...

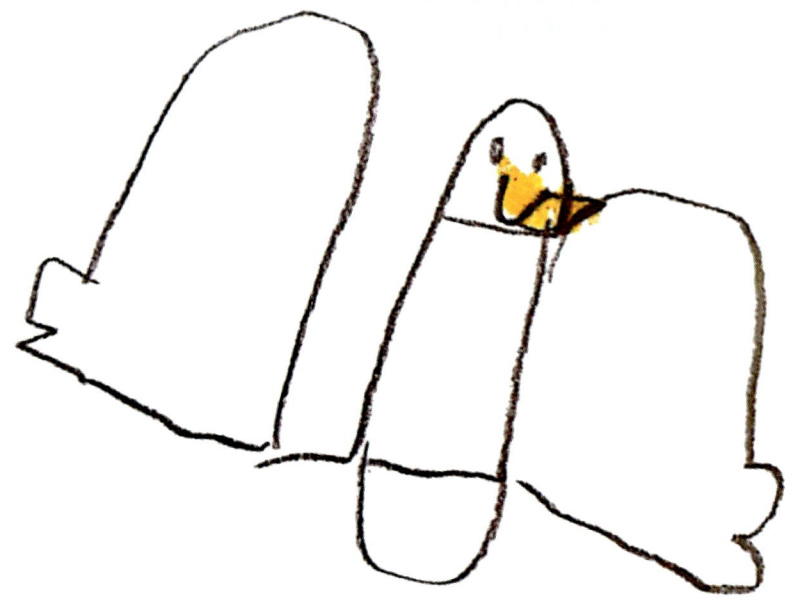

John the Baptist told many people about Jesus and baptized them with water. He even baptized Jesus! And when He did the Holy Spirit fell upon Jesus like a dove.

After his baptism, as Jesus came up out of the water, the heavens were opened and he saw the Spirit of God descending like a dove and settling on him.

Matthew 3:16 NLT

Because of LOVE...

40

Jesus did not eat for forty days and forty nights and was tempted by the devil in the wilderness.

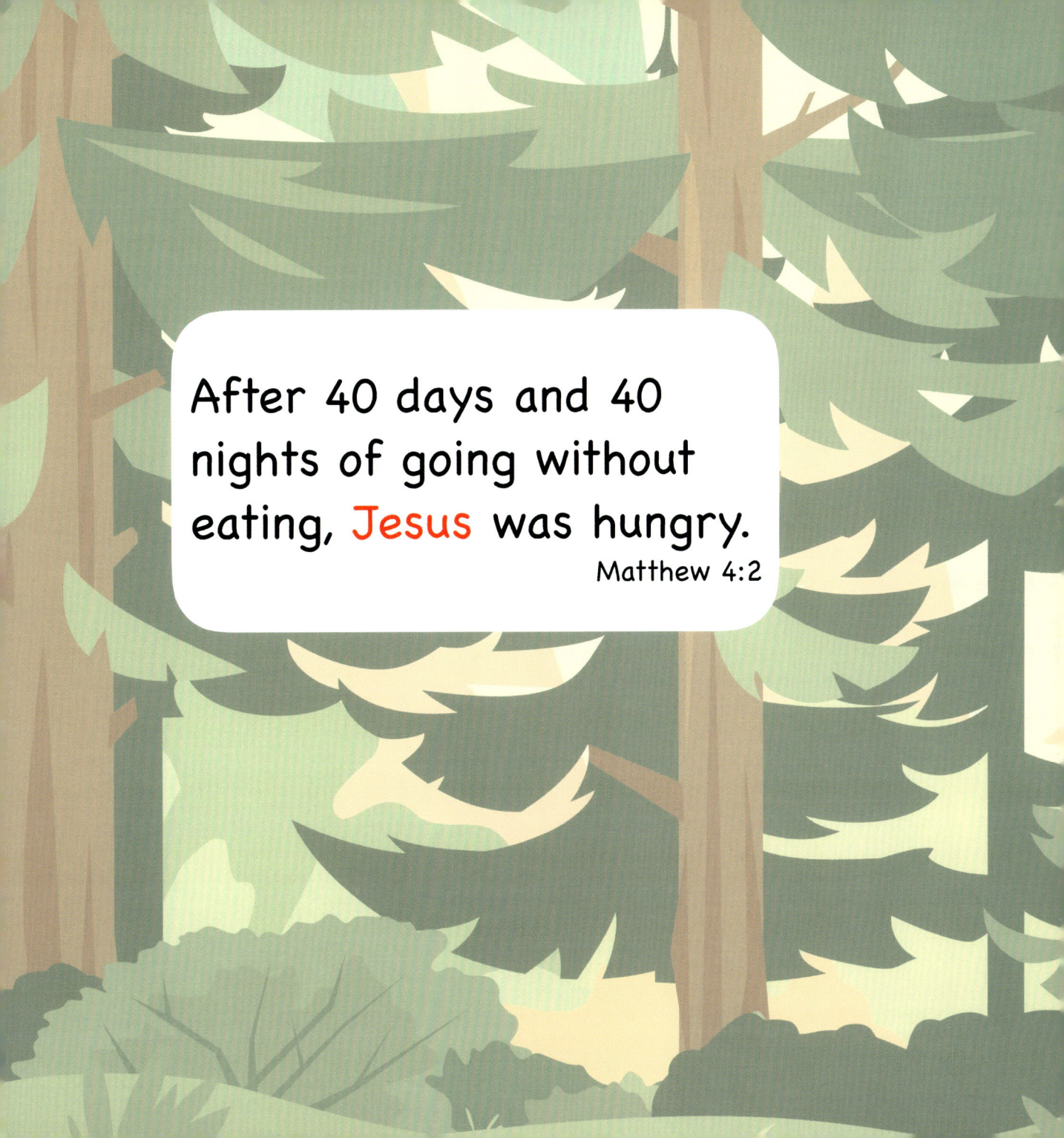

After 40 days and 40 nights of going without eating, Jesus was hungry.

Matthew 4:2

Because of LOVE...

Jesus began to preach about God and teach people how to live. He called disciples to come and follow Him too.

Here are the names of the 12 apostles. First there were Simon Peter and his brother Andrew. Then came James, son of Zebedee, and his brother John. Next were Philip and Bartholomew, and also Thomas and Matthew the tax collector. Two more were James, son of Alphaeus, and Thaddaeus. The last were Simon the Zealot and Judas Iscariot.

Matthew 10:2-4

Because of LOVE...

Jesus healed many people, those who were sick, or blind, or could not walk. He also gave food to thousands of people.

A vast crowd brought to him people who were lame, blind, crippled, those who couldn't speak, and many others. They laid them before Jesus, and he healed them all.

Matthew 15:30 NLT

Then he took the seven loaves and the fish, thanked God for them, and broke them into pieces. He gave them to the disciples, who distributed the food to the crowd.

Matthew 15:36 NLT

Because of LOVE...

Jesus ate with the disciples. He blessed the bread to represent His body, and the drink to represent His blood.

While they were eating, Jesus took bread. He gave thanks and broke it. He handed it to his disciples and said, "Take this and eat it. This is my body."

Matthew 26:26

Because of LOVE...

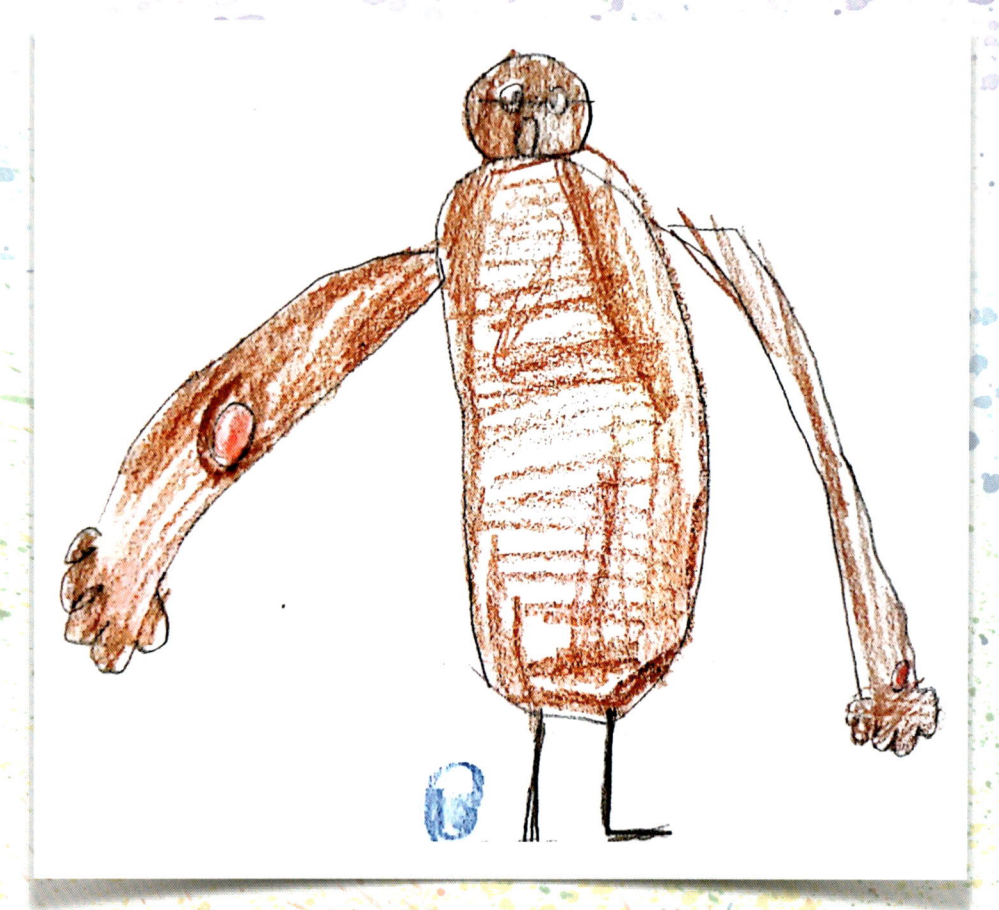

Jesus prayed for God's will to be done, even though it would cause Him great pain.

Jesus went away a second time. He prayed, "My Father, is it possible for this cup to be taken away? But if I must drink it, may what you want be done."

Matthew 26:42

Because of LOVE...

Jesus allowed a crowd of men to take Him. He knew the disciple, Judas, would betray Him.

So Judas went to Jesus at once. He said, "Greetings, Rabbi!" And he kissed him. Jesus replied, "Friend, do what you came to do." Then the men stepped forward. They grabbed Jesus and arrested him.

Matthew 26:49-50

Because of LOVE...

Jesus endured being treated very badly even though He had done nothing wrong.

"What do you think?" "He must die!" they answered. Then they spit in his face. They hit him with their fists. Others slapped him.

Matthew 26:66-67

Because of LOVE...

Jesus was nailed to the cross. He forgave those who mistreated Him even while He was on the cross.

Jesus said, "Father, forgive them, for they don't know what they are doing." And the soldiers gambled for his clothes by throwing dice.

Luke 23:34 NLT

Because of LOVE...

A man named Joseph put cloth on Jesus and laid Him in a new tomb. He rolled a stone in front of it.

Joseph took the body and wrapped it in a clean linen cloth. He placed it in his own new tomb that he had cut out of the rock. He rolled a big stone in front of the entrance to the tomb. Then he went away.

Matthew 27:59-60

Because of LOVE... 3

Jesus remained in the tomb for three days. But on the third day, He rose from the dead!

Then the angel spoke to the women. "Don't be afraid!" he said. "I know you are looking for Jesus, who was crucified. He isn't here! He is risen from the dead, just as he said would happen. Come, see where his body was lying."

Matthew 28:5-6 NLT

Because of Love...

Jesus appeared to the disciples before He was taken up to heaven. God left them the Holy Spirit as promised.

When the Lord Jesus had finished talking with them, he was taken up into heaven and sat down in the place of honor at God's right hand.

Mark 16:19 NLT

Because of Love...

The disciples continued to preach and teach, and heal many people through the power of the Holy Spirit and the authority of Jesus Christ.

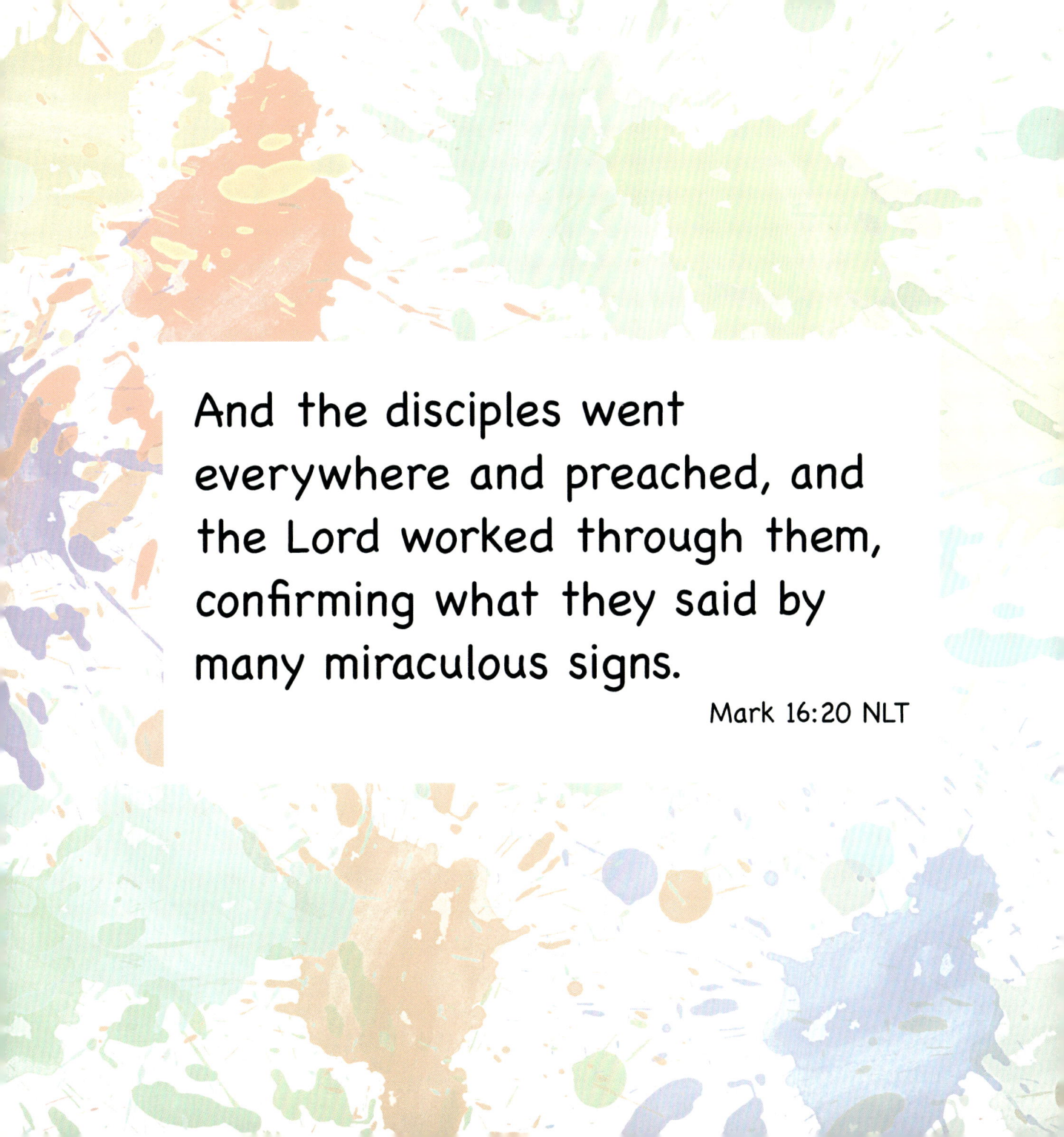

And the disciples went everywhere and preached, and the Lord worked through them, confirming what they said by many miraculous signs.

Mark 16:20 NLT

Because of Love...

The message of salvation through faith in Jesus Christ continues to be shared today. We can receive God's free gift of salvation if we believe.

"...The message is very close at hand; it is on your lips and in your heart." And that message is the very message about faith that we preach. If you confess with your mouth that Jesus is Lord and believe in your heart that God raised Jesus from the dead, you will be saved.

Romans 10:8-9 NLT

Epilogue

Now that you have read this love story, you may be thinking, "What does this mean for me?"

This means that God loves YOU

God knew we needed a perfect sacrifice to pay the price for our sin (wrongdoing). So He gave His one and only Son, Jesus, so we might have life eternally (John 3:16). That's how much He loves us. That's how much He loves YOU.

He wants you to experience His perfect love (1 John 4:18).
He wants you to know Him just as He knows you (John 10:14).
He wants you to be with Him forever, in eternity (1 John 5:11).

God wants YOU, and when you are ready to receive Him into your heart and make Him a part of your life, you can pray this simple prayer:

God,
I know that I have done wrong. I have not done what pleases You and I am sorry. I ask for Your forgiveness and that You make my heart clean. I believe that Jesus died on the cross for my sins and that You raised Jesus from the dead. I confess that Jesus Christ is Lord and I accept Him into my heart as my Savior (the One who saved me from my sin) and my Lord (the Master of my life). Thank You Lord for saving me.

In Jesus' Name. Amen.

About the Author

Damitra Newsome is a wife, mother, educator, and an overall creative. She holds an advanced degree in mathematics (her favorite subject) and has spent over 10 years in the public school system serving students, teachers, and families in various roles. When she is not serving in this capacity, she enjoys crafting, natural hair braiding, jigsaw puzzles, and singing praise and worship at her local church. "Because of Love" is her first published book, and it is near and dear to her heart. She believes discipleship begins at home and that she and her husband have been given an assignment by God to share the Good News with their daughter, Kaycie, as well as other families.

About the Illustrator

Kaycie Newsome is a fun-loving and energetic, five-year-old girl who loves legos, drawing, swimming, and technology (her favorite subject). She enjoys discussing facts about all things space and researching facts about the human body and other subjects she finds interesting. In her quiet time, she can be found reading a good book to herself or to her stuffed animals. She also enjoys reading children's mystery books with her dad (oh the suspense!). Kaycie has big dreams for her future, including becoming an astronaut, teacher, and space engineer.

Published in the USA

**SoAllMayKnow
PUBLISHING** ™

ISBN 978-1-7347064-2-0